Emma Steel

To Carry A Flame

Emma Steel was born in Devon, England. She began writing in her late teens but didn't start to publish work until later in life. She moved to the States in the mid-nineties where she worked for many years, writing stories in her spare time.
In early 2025, she began to write poetry, in addition to her short story work, writing an eclectic blend of light and dark poems that weave memories of the past and fantasy together. She started to work with Write Angle Publishing at the end of 2025 to bring them to print.

To Carry A Flame

by Emma Steel

Write Angle Publishing
Earleville, MD
www.writeanglepublishing.com

To Carry A Flame
Copyright © 2026 Emma Steel
Published by Write Angle Publishing
Earleville, MD

Emma Steel, Author

All works in this collection have been printed with the permission of the author.
All rights reserved.
No portion of this publication may be reproduced, stored in any electronic system, copied or transmitted in any form or by any means, electronic, digital, mechanical, photocopy, recording or otherwise without the written permission of the author. This includes any storage of the authors work on an information storage and retrieval system.
Any resemblance to any actual person, living or dead, or to any location is the coincidental invention of the author's creative mind.

ISBN: 978-1-971249-03-2

CONTENTS

Be My Sun	3
Salvation's Song	4
Sunday Mornings	5
Loving Tree	6
The Vampire's Kiss	7
Grasping	8
Love Lotto	9
Enough	10
Blue Sky	11
True Love	12
The Challenge	14
Smile	15
Words	15
Reborn	16
Jewels In The Sky	17
Choose Well	18
The Law	19
Subtlety	20
A Lessor Goddess	21
Hush	22
Snow	23
Goddess	24
Hammock	26
Moments	27
The Tower	28
Stardust	29
Filling The Void	30

Moon	32
Breath	34
Clockwork Heart	34
Fruit	35
The Taste of Love	36
Bring Me Love	38
Surrender	40
Emergency!	41
Tears	42
Angel	43
Romance	44
A World At My Fingertips	46
When Winter Comes	48
Acceptance of Each Other	50
Sisters	51
Friendship	52
How?	54
Language	55
Breakfast Treats	56
The Tree	58
Tomorrow's Memories	60
My Kind of People	62
Flaming June	64
Treasure	65
A Glimmer of Hope	66
Hungry	67
The Long Road	68
X Marks the Spot	69
A Pause in Chores	70
Lantern	71

Tears for You	72
Make Me Want You!	73
My Friend of the Moon	74
Prayers	75
Terra Firma	76
You are my Empress	78
Songs	79
I Can't	80
Curses and Prayers	82
Meet me in Eternity	84
Burning for You	86
The Last Doves	87
Colors	88
The Mirror Has No Glass	90
Gothic Beauty	92
You Saved Me	94
Sacrifice	95
The Ship	96
Wind	98
The Effects of Love	100
The Summer Isles	102
The Shield	104
Fingerprints	105
Heartbeat	106
Summer	107

To Carry A Flame

Be My Sun

When the night passes
I want my day in the sun
Who shines brightly in my eyes
Leaves her mark on my pale skin
Warms me to the core
And is a beacon to follow
    when I am uncertain

There is a sun out there
That shines brighter than the others
It is not a case of proximity
Or the light that is closest, shines brightest
It is a need for the right light
The one you can stare at without going blind

The sun that sets fire to you
When you get close
Her gravity that pulls you in
Refusing to relinquish you
And you stay in her orbit forever
Be that sun

Salvation's Song

Sing little bird
With your feathers bright,
Bring the light back into the world,
On a high note, so sweet.

Paint a picture with your song,
Of hope and peace,
A world of sun and warmth
    for thee and me,
Salvation's song.

Sunday Mornings

A kiss
It's only the sun

A caress
It's only the sun

To feel the warmth
It's only the sun

Laid in bed on a lazy Sunday
Snuggled under the soft covers

Wishing you were here
And not only the sun

Loving Tree

My love is like a tree
A small seedling, barely poking
    through the soil
Getting stronger as it grows,
    reaching for the sky

My love is like a tree
Trunk strong, sturdy
Supporting many branches

My love is like a tree
Its foliage shades from harsh sun
Giving comfort to those with me

My love is like a tree
Hug me
Climb me

The Vampire's Kiss

Her neck arched back,
As she pulled away long hair,
Exposing the slender, milky skin.

A blue green vein pulsed,
Full with life,
And tempting.

The temptation
Of life,
Too much.

Glistening teeth,
Bright white,
Tainted red as they sink.

Two lovers,
Sharing one life,
As the vampire kisses.

Grasping

Hold my hand
Fingers entwined
As they grip tight
So my knuckles turn white
Exquisite pain

You let my hands go
I want your grip
But you need them
To delight

I clutch the sheets
Twisting in place
Pinned aggressively
Wild, but consenting
Until I am spent

Love Lotto

The sun was up before me,
a common occurrence.
Sleep fills my eyes,
a cat strokes my legs,
tail held high.
"Feed me,"
it demands.
Everyone demands.
But what about me?
When do I get mine?
Perhaps yesterday was a
failure?
What am I striving for?
Affection?
Love?
Today is another chance.

Enough

Vaulted ceilings
Risen from stone walls
Laden with decoration
Strong and rich

Gardens of grass
And ornamental shrubs
That meander like a maze
A world of rare delights

But I would live in cardboard
If you were here
Shrouding me with your arms
You are enough

Blue Sky

I wandered through the sky,
Blue and bright,
Spring-like days that
Banish mists and clouds.

The air is fresh,
The voices clear.
Eyes shine with a sparkle,
Minds alike.

In the arms
Of those who read,
With minds open and free,
There are companionship and love.

True Love

There is a sadness that lives in us all
Small, frightened, and curled up
Bitter tears leak from its eyes, unseen
But they are felt by each who is its prison

A small vulnerability that we defend
Hiding from the world for fear of discovery
Thrashing out at those who approach
For we fear the pain that exposure brings

Seek the one who can tend to your sadness
Lift it to the light
Wash it with delicate strokes
And clothe it in soft linens

To find the love of our lives
Frees us from the pain of sadness
If only we can learn to let go
Of the sadness we harbor

Do not fight love, tenderness,
But let it into your life
Learn to accept love
Learn to accept freedom

For only you have the power
To be open and willing
To accept salvation through
True Love

The Challenge

My shell is hard, tough, and resilient
Built layer upon layer of the hardest stone
A shield to protect what is inside
The softest part of me, vulnerable
It resists hammer blows, the heat of a torch
And all manner of withering stare and harsh words
But there are cracks, leakage at the edges
The soft trail of fingers tips
The touch of lips, gentle and tender
The feel of your breath on my skin
Making fine hairs rise, head thrown back
My resolve dissolves under your gaze
How can I deny you anything?
I am crumbling, please, catch the pieces

Smile

Where there was once ice
Now there is fire
Heavens ablaze
Our feet planted in rich soil
We seek to grow
Toward the jewel strewn firmament
That we might give those jewels to another
For just a smile

Words

Reading poetry
Words slide through my eyes
They work their magic
Soothing the mind
Enflaming the heart
In each letter and syllable
There is a piece of you
That I almost taste
Each word is delicious

Reborn

Your presence is enough,
Here beside me,
As I release the pain held tightly,
Allowing to it flow free.
Exposed and vulnerable
To only you,
For I know that your love,
Holding true, cures.
The light you bring
Burns away the shadows,
Revealing my core,
My Heart,
My soul,
All that is me in its purest form.
There is nothing I would deny you,
As we merge together,
I am more than I was,
Under your touch -
Soothing and cool,
Against my burning flesh.
Seared by my past
Undone by those before,
But with you,
I am reborn, fresh, and renewed.

In The Sky

Dance and weave as we move to the music
    of the spheres
The stars in the velvet darkness
Tease the necklace they would make
Those jewels just out of reach
But were we together
They would be but trinkets
Compared to us

I will watch them burn
One by one, going out
Before I would relinquish you
Each jewel less than your countenance
Close to me
In your presence
There is no darkness

Choose Well

Love opens you up,
Exposing your heart,
Cracked and broken,
Pieces scattered on the road
To self-discovery.

When you look to memories and smile,
Build those memories with someone,
Who, when you look back,
You want to still to be there –

And when you turn your head,
They are.

The Law

We are quantum entangled
However far apart
In complete harmony
So that when you move close
Every atom in me vibrates
Every pore perspires
Like a breath from my entire body
And there is a sound that comes from me
That only you can hear
Under silk and cotton
The Universe dictates that
I cannot deny it
It is the Law

Subtlety

Subtlety is the enemy of action
A glance
A well-placed word
The brush of a hand on an arm
All designed to bring two closer
But perhaps, subtlety stands guardian
Like cling film, a micro thin barrier
Thwarting intent unless obvious
How to break the distance
When it is so small
Almost indivisible
No weak point
Except the lips

A Lessor Goddess

Broken, I lay after her ministrations
Wanton still, craving her taste
Lips parted in a whisper
Commanding my attention and my moves

Traffic with a muse is two-way
A give and a take
She sets the rules, and others obey
Or the gifts are withdrawn

She has no concern for my frame
My body, my mind
She wants what she wants
And will take all, and I give

Such is her right,
This lessor Goddess
Everlasting, daughter of Zeus
I belong to her, entirely

Hush

Hush.
Rest that fevered mind
That speaks false.
There is love in you for a reason,
Seek not any taker,
Rather, those that will cherish.
Guard jealously that love,
For that which has no cost,
Has no value.
Extract a toll for your gifts,
They are to be earned,
Worked for, slaved for,
And not discarded quickly.
I value you, sweet girl
I see you, and your worth.

Snow

Each flake falling, unique.
Crystalized water like a captured dream,
floating before my eyes and bringing
such delight.
Our mittens are crusted white as we play.
Drifts against the side of every building
make them seem as though they grew
from the ground, organically.
When winter comes, I love it.
The way that it makes your cheeks flush,
flakes on your eyelashes,
and the smile you throw
makes all the shovelling worth it.
I would shovel the world
for a smile from you.

Goddess

Sometimes your blood just runs faster, your heart beats hard and there is a guttural sound within you that needs to be let loose. Today, I am on fire, you need to help me quench it, set it free. Let it burn wild, the heat that has been restrained for too long, so that it can then be constrained again for a while.

I see you, legs either side of me, straddling my midriff, as I lay beneath you, wrists pinned, but not struggling. Our eyes are locked as you lean over me, the skin on your stomach rippled as it folds, just like the sheets that lay crumbled around us on the bed. I can smell you, a fragrance that sets me ablaze.

I love your eyes, locking my attention. The way your pupils dilate when you look at me, the way the creases curve when you laugh, matching the shape of your eyes, and the sparkle you always have in them. You are so beautiful that it makes me hurt, and I feel unworthy.

But sometimes a girl just needs to get fucked, hard. Taken so that she has no other option but to submit to your fingers, your mouth. Your lips push into me hard, smashing my mouth, and I wonder if the bruises will be noticeable when we have broken, and you set me free for the day.

You tease, breasts pressed against me, so that it seems we share skin. Your hands explore every inch of me, making a roadmap for your mouth that marks its trail with your lips and tongue, alternately kissing and licking so that my skin is wet under you.

I love you so much, would do anything for you, commit any sin, and you force me to prove it. Taking me with your fingers before you kiss me gently at first, then more aggressively as you savor my flavor. My body responds, arching and aching at the same time as a tension builds.

The energy cannot be held, and I growl, the sound starting in my chest, rolling as it works its way up to my throat, forcing every muscle to tense on its way until it rumbles from lips that snarl like a tiger in heat, snapping and biting her mate, but I cannot bite, I can only hold your head in my hands.

I grip your skull, pulling your hair, as I guide it to where the feeling is almost too intense. You work, kissing, lapping, probing with mouth, tongue, and fingers, moving between each based on my reaction. With eyes rolled back, my hands clasp and release, my grip hard.

I worship at your altar, a generous Goddess who gives me gifts, sacrificing myself. Gifts of pleasure, sometimes pain, whatever your desire is. My body is flushed, my chest red, my skin itchy, and there is a release of pleasure that ripples over me, wave after wave as my release comes.

Hammock

Dappled sunshine covers my naked skin, forcing freckles to the surface as though the color boiled just beneath, waiting to be set free. The hammock swings gently as I lay, snug in the curve, cocooned in cotton. The ribs of the netting mark me so that when I have had enough, I will bear them as a reminder for a short while.

The air is still, and the earth holds her breath, reluctant to disturb my peace on this spring day. My mind needs the peace, and I am grateful as I watch a cloud drift, blown on a wind at high altitude, chasing a plane's vapor trail in play. If only I could join it, taking to the air, flying - arms outstretched.

The world seems too small, closing in on me, a box that shrinks every day. Yesterday it was so large, room to explore, to walk, to run, and never see the same thing twice. To travel the world hand in hand with a partner in crime; challenging norms and carrying each other.

The hammock rests in a strong frame, strong enough to bear two. Take the weight from your feet, come lay in the sun with me, and I will share the space with you. There is sun enough for both of us and let me trace my fingers over the diamonds that the mesh makes on you as we explore the world, and each other together.

Moments

There was a moment when I fell so deep
that I didn't know when I hit the bottom,
unable to get up, curled on the floor.
The cold tiles pressed into soft flesh
and bitter tears rolled from red eyes.
Black lines seared into my cheeks,
carried on salty water.

There was a moment when I was resurrected,
lifted from blackness and brought to the light.
I could feel the sun once more, feel joy,
as I took your proffered hand and drew myself up,
borrowing your strength.
When I did so, all I could think was
I want to drown in the moment,
And you are that moment for me.

The Tower

I sit in my tower of stone,
grey, solid, and impenetrable,
overlooking the landscape below me,
all ashes.

The world has burned, and I am here,
locked in stone, apart from all others,
body and mind broken.
I am left holding the matches.

I built this tower myself.
I laid one step at a time,
climbing higher and higher,
removing the steps as I went.

Now, there is no way down, lost in isolation.
Comfortable in the prison I built,
surrounded by the items I furnished.
Reminders of a life once lived,
    now just memories.

I am no Rapunzel, but I often wonder
if there is not some Princess
that could not at least lend me
a ladder!

Stardust

A million, million years ago there was a star
   that shone
Hanging in the night sky, bright was its light
Showing itself to all who looked,
Though there was no one here to see it

When it collapsed, it cast itself out
Crossing galaxies and the vastness of space
Traveling through time, the hard way
Never stopping

Material can neither created nor destroyed
And everything is reused, recycled
And so, some of it became you
Sitting in the darkness on the bed

I see you, your skin, warm to the touch
Like a star that still burns under my fingers
Spinning and turning, full of energy
And when I look into your eyes I recognize
   what you were those long years ago

You still have your fire
You still captivate me, glowing
And I am lost in your vastness
As I give myself to the night

Filling The Void

inside me, there is a hole
as large as a cavern,
a hole that can't be filled
or accessed
from the outside,
I have tried.

the casual laughter,
quick glances broken,
the eyes that lock only briefly,
the hands that do not touch,
all fall short
too thin a feeling to stay.

seeping away quickly
as the void remains,
as deep and empty as ever,
I want, no need,
a love as thick as honey
that seeps slowly.

sticky on the fingers,
slick to the touch,
to share with someone
who shares the taste,
discriminating,
luscious.

we would share
the world,
pleasure and pain,
thick and thin,
as we filled the void
in each other.

each day, teaming,
for support and success,
can there be finer
than to be with
the person who
completes you,

completely.

Moon

i show my face at night
pale, distant, and beautiful
on different nights,
i will show a different face
each an aspect of me

ancient, but ever-present
i tease from afar
it seems you could touch me
when you hold out your hand
but i am always just out of reach

i create tides that pull you to me
and push you away alternately
predictable in the month
as I ebb and flow
awash in emotion

i am the bringer of magic
bestowing my gifts
delicious and rare
on those who are worthy
and capable of wielding them

you love to watch me
imagining yourself with me
but when the curtains are drawn
and the sky is hidden
you will never see me coming

Breath

share my breath
seal this compact with a kiss
because
you already live in my mind
and after i gave you my heart
you stole my soul
so
take the rest of me

Clockwork Heart

Sixty ticks a minute
Never Fast
Never Slow
Beating like clockwork
Until the end of time
So, wind it up
My love
And try
To make it race

Fruit

Sweet as honey, and just as sticky.
I lick my lips as the juices escape,
a dribble on my chin as I relish the flavor.

Warm, like the sun you capture,
coalesced sunshine made solid
by the body.

There is a tremble as my tongue
covers the surface, feeling the texture,
the soft innards as it probes.

A gasp escapes lips,
a light hum that vibrates sending
sensations through my lips

The sweetest of summer fruits
laid bare and taken in the summer
is a treasure to behold and be enjoyed.

The Taste of Love

Do you remember the taste of love?

Does it linger, as sweet in your memories as it was on your tongue, a drink you could never get your fill of, so that every fiber of your body ached and was distended by its presence?

Or is it bitter, mocking, and soured by the hurt done in its name? A falsehood that tore your heart from your body, burning it before your eyes with a smile on the face of the one who did it?

There is no doubt; regardless, it leaves a stain on the lips, a mark that cannot be washed away by soap or time. Its flavor may mellow, but it will linger long past any expiration date printed on a milk carton.

This liquid becomes a natural fiber spun by a spider. Its web is designed to capture us, holding us until we can be consumed. Enticed by the intricate designs of an hourglass, its sting is painful and long-lasting.

Or could it be a caterpillar wrapping itself in silk, which it will share with you as fine clothes? Delicate silks, soft on the skin, are the result of its transformation. Molding itself into something that you marvel at with each glance of the iridescent wings.

For me, love drips through me like honey from a spoon, oozing slowly, running over my soul, sticky on the fingers I lick clean with you still in my mind. I hear your voice, even though we have never met and you don't know I exist today, but one day providence will bring us together, some weird twist that fate has planned, but yet to share...

Bring Me Love

when love finds me again, removing the shelter i hid myself in, that comfortable safety; i want it to announce itself loudly. there should be no skirting the edge of the light in shame, but a celebration.

i want days of passion and tender longing that span time. even as it grows, there should still be a passion. even anger can end in a kind word and a gentle touch, soft-spoken feelings that soothe the heat from it and a reconciliation that is heartfelt, not demanded.

i want to eat my fill, until i can consume no more, but still hunger for you. to be the first thing i see when the light filters into our room, and the last as your body is painted in peach and lilac light as the sun drowns behind the trees.

i want to love and be loved. not drag out life in an easy prison with someone, neither wanting to leave because the other knows where the bodies are buried. love is a gift to be shared through both times of plenty and times of famine; both should eat from its plate.

love is not the avoidance of mutually assured destruction, but the feeling that together, there is nothing that cannot be overcome, even if we have nothing. each of us, is more than enough for the other.

bring me this shining gift - no box required to pack it in, no gold, no silver - and it will be payment enough for me. I cannot be bought, but I will willingly give myself to one who I love and who loves me truly.

Surrender

There is fear in your eyes and
Every muscle shakes
In ecstasy and terror
As your body explodes with pleasure
At the realization that
She merely rents room in your head
But lives in your soul
Because you are
Completely hers

Emergency!

She was driving, cars passing on either side.
Her voice mirrored the song on the radio,
The sun, shining in her hair,
Her lips moving in pleasure,
At the delight of the music.

Pull over!
She questioned me with, "Why?"
"Just do it, it's an emergency!" I told her.
On the hard shoulder, she looked at me,
Questioning eyes that melt me every time.

Everything about this girl
Made me want her, desperately,
"What's so urgent?" she asked.
I cupped her face between my hands,
Leaning toward her, eyes locked.

"I have to kiss you, right now."
Lips met, sinking deeply into the moment,
Cars continuing to pass us,
As seconds ran slowly, elongated.
"Otherwise, I might die," I told her.

Tears

I see you crying
Sobbing gently into the night
And it breaks my heart
Let me take the tears
Treasure each one
Wipe them with my thumb
Kiss them from your cheek
Tasting their salt, tasting of you

Tears can be cried for many reasons
From fear, hate, anger, or sorrow
I want to wrap you in my arms
Enfolded in safety and protected
From this bitter world
So that from this day forth
When tears flow from you
They do so only in joy or passion

Angel

if i become an angel
it will be because they relaxed
the entrance exam
or i stole in the back

my wings will be grubby
not the white of everyone else's
but that's the way i like it
if it's a sin, i'm in

where is the fun
in never doing anything?
you have to live
before you die

Romance

love isn't all night times and negligees

it is the whisper in the day, a private moment in public

it is picking up sticks together when one disappears, returning with a mug of tea, steaming contents soon inside you and paid for with a kiss under the plum tree while you rest together

it is knowing that she will be there, waiting, while you are away, and when you return her lips will be on yours before the bags hit the floor

it is wearing a smile rather than a scowl, not because you are hiding the scowl in moments of frustration, but because even then, you know who you have

it is about arguing, but making amends even when you were right, just because you don't ever want her to be wrong; and she feels the same

it is not just about the touch of skin under the sheets, but the placement of your hand on her leg when you are out, and hers on yours it is about adoring the color of her eyes, and even when you are still looking at them, it is as if it is the first time you have seen them, watching her lips move as she talks

it is about being together at the same time, and present, because of all the places you could be, and the people you could be with, this is the only place that feels right

it is about sitting still while she softly ties a ribbon in your hair, because she wanted to see you that way

it is about showing the yearning you have for her, while she is still holding your hand

it is about kissing ice cream from her lips, but knowing she tastes better

romance isn't some grand gesture; it is woven into everything you do together, and apart, for the one you *love*

A World At My Fingertips

On the Serengeti, the trees stand tall, but flattened, as if matching the landscape. The grasslands range for hundreds of miles in each direction, peppered by watering holes like sesame seeds on a bun. All manner of wildlife roam, at easy leisure, except for the occasional chase where a predator will take down its prey in the circle of life.

In Greece, the temples dot the countryside. Stone monuments that harken back to the dawn of civilization, places where the Gods once deigned to cohort with mortals, giving them gifts, prophetic answers through their seers, and raining down justice upon them.

In Iceland, surrounded by volcanoes and snow, what grass grows is short to protect itself from the cold. The days can be long or short depending on the time of year. At night, the sky will be extra black, so dark that the pinpricks of light that are our Milky Way peer like a chick from the nest, but at certain times the sky becomes a wonder. Shot through with color, greens, reds, and blues waving above, a galactic lightshow unmatched by any man can create.

I sit here on a sofa tufted with oxblood red leather, created in an old style. The room is dim, with curtains drawn to keep the bright sun out. Even during the day, a lamp on a side table gives a yellow light that provides comfort and atmosphere. The furniture is made of black walnut, matched with the streaky pattern of wormy maple, dark marks on white wood.

Of all the places I could be, why am I here, in this room, instead of among those wondrous and mysterious places? Because this is where you are, sitting next to me, bare feet on the coffee table.

How are they supposed to compete with you?

When Winter Comes

When winter comes and the trees stand bare and still like skeletons of dead wood

When winter comes and the wind blows, trying to steal your flesh from your bones with teeth of steel

When winter comes and the holly is the only green left, red berries peeking out in defiance

When winter comes and the ground gets hard as rock, and the puddles all frozen lakes of trapped air

When winter comes and the roads are icy skating rinks for the cars that slid as they pass

When winter comes and we wear our thick underwear that we both laugh about

When winter comes and you don the heavy coat that is too large, the one that looks like a sleeping bag

When winter comes and your cheeks are flushed red and your lips chap, so they are rough when we kiss

When winter comes and we sit by the fire with hot chocolate, staring at the flames in the long evenings together

When winter comes, hold me softly, and keep me warm until Spring, my love, so that we can bloom together and make love under the new sun

Acceptance of Each Other

Sundays are reserved for communion,
for some that means a seat in the church,
for others it means with nature on a walk,
for some it means quiet time with a loved one,
and others still surrounded by family.

To those who read this on that day,
a confluence of day and meaning,
who accept someone into their thoughts
not knowing them, except by their words and actions
I send you my love.

Because, regardless of how we love,
we know that the divine does not make mistakes,
only creates opportunities
for us to accept other,
in support of the divine message.

Whoever you follow,
and however you seek communion,
may peace by with you,
and I love you with a true spirit.

Sisters

Dapples patch the lawn as the sun breaks through the trees.

There is light enough for all on a bright day, but on a cloudy one, we must share our light with others, as they share theirs with us, when our sun is covered.

An umbrella is big enough for all; offer cover during the storm - the shelter is welcome. No one should stand in the rain alone.

Give a warm hearth in times of need. Tea or coffee, and an ear, can soothe the mind and the soul. Food is about more than food, it is caring.

We are stronger when we stand hand in hand, caring for one another, taking the weight we each bear. I feel your hands in mine, and I know that I am safe.

There is a brace for my broken spirit, a splint for my wings, and you give me the space to heal until I can fly again, and when I do, I will dedicate the air to you as I soar.

We can look to the skies, but we are each other's blessings, sisters together.

Friendship

How can you make the world both larger and smaller at the same time?

Is it some kind of magic?

The world seems to grow, a more expansive place filled with opportunities - chances to sit and converse, share a drink, and smile.

An easy afternoon spent in delightful company, friends enjoying each other's company as though all was right with the world.

Yet, you also make the world smaller - cozy, comfortable, not frightening, like a small cottage parlor, where everything is crowded around you in the knowledge that it is all familiar and safe.

These two states co-exist in my world, a flight of fancy secure in the knowledge that I am free to fly, to reach for the heights of what is achievable, because I know if I fall, you will catch me.

This gives me the strength to try everything and take the risks that I am frightened to attempt, in short, you make me a better woman for your friendship.

How?

Your fingers slowly trace my skin, and I twist in pleasure as I feel them, samite over satin.

My skin tingles as you move the ice cube, drawing it in a line, small circles, leaving a trail of wetness behind it as you draw up my stomach and between my breasts, placing small kisses upon the line so that drops form on your lips.

When the ice cube reaches my nipple, it peaks, hard, fruitlessly trying to rebel when I have already collapsed.

You pop the ice cube in your mouth, wet cherry lips close around it as it disappears, rolled by your tongue in darkness and unseen, but we both know it is there.

How? How do you make me melt like an ice cube as you hold my eyes with yours, before you threaten me with a good time?

Language

Kind words tumble from soft lips.
Floating through the mind,
Weaving between neurons.
They leave a trail, a pathway,
But language is fickle,
Often misunderstood.
It can be kind or harsh,
Unforgiving or incredibly supportive.
Words bind stronger than steel, softer than silk,
Do we speak the same tongue?

Breakfast Treats

Cherries chopped, halved, and ready
The morning light will filter in through the kitchen window
The coffee pot will be full, the gurgle set off automatically
Slowly I weigh flour, one ounce, then two, etc., until complete
Sugar will follow
Each ingredient added to the mix while the oven preheats
Hot, it will radiate, filling the kitchen with an urgency
I start to get excited as I flatten out the mix
Patting it like a good child in praise
Before separating the pieces
Gently arranging them on a baking sheet lined with parchment paper
The rack will grate, a scraping sound as the tray is slid into place
And the wait begins…
Even before the treats are finished, I can smell them
Too early to eat, but my mouth prepares
Like I anticipate a lover, waiting for her
Watching her ready and preen
But this is determined by a timer and sight
When I judge them done, I remove them
The air fills with their scent, strong, sweet

And I am filled with a longing, testing my resolve
They slide onto the rack to cool - ten minutes, I can wait
They are still warm as I draw one on to a plate
Butter melts into the soft, fluffy scone as I spread the yellow
And savor the reward
If only everything were so simple, and so pleasurable

The Tree

The last time I saw the tree, the bark was cracked and dry, the branches withered, crooked, and my heart sank at its dying.

There was a hole in the truck, the edges torn and rotting. Some creature had made a home of it, the tree giving a last vestige of use before some wind would come and finally tear it down.

The tree might have stood in this spot for centuries, a landmark for others who passed by, using it to find their way to other places, never stopping to look, or paying mind to the tree.

Once the road had been laid, time was lost to the tree; there was no longer time to stand and stare. The cars passed at forty miles an hour, never stopping.

I had known this tree my whole life, it had watched me grow in the days before the road, when a person could hang ropes from it and swing, climb its limbs, and pretend to play forts before being told girls don't do that.

I felt like the tree's death had stolen part of my childhood, a tenuous connection to lost summers, and I could feel the welling of salty tears at the thought of it.

My heart lifted as I walked around it, trailing my fingertips over the rough surface. Green shoots from the roots burst forth, breaking the soil and reaching for the sky above them.

I was broken, a smile played across my lips, and the tears still fell, but for happier reasons, as I recognized that life is not over just because life looks stopped, it continues to push us forward.

I learned a lesson that day, that however poor things look, there is a future, you just need to be standing in the right place to see it.

Tomorrow's Memories

Do you remember that time when we made a tent fort from the sheets? Laying together under the beige cotton so that the light filtered through was colored and faint like the light that passes over a pond in winter.

The morning we played? Laid, just watching each other breathe, the movement of every muscle, the color of your eyes, and the way your hair lay on the pillow.

The excitement at doing nothing was so palpable I could feel my skin tingle, and when you trailed your fingers over my hip, it was as if you were wired to the mains and passing the current to me.

Do you remember the morning in the kitchen? I frothed milk and poured it over the espresso so that the latte looked like a pool that we could both dive into. The foam settled on your top lip as you drew on the large cup, and I laughed as you pretended to be Chaplin at his height.

The music played through the speaker, and we held each other as we just swayed to the beat, no one else around, just you and I in the kitchen, a morning drenched in pleasure and joy at the simple things in life.

Do you remember those memories?

I do. I carry them with me for us and wait for you so that we can experience them together; and then, one day, when we look back, we can both smile at the thought of the memories we made together and share.

I look forward to nuzzling your neck while you cut vegetables at the counter, or your arms around my waist as I wash a cup at the sink, giving you a kiss as I turn for the drying cloth.

Life is made of the small moments, and the beauty of small moments is that you can fit so many of them in the same space, crammed tight with happy memories as we merge our lives together.

My Kind of People

I'm a simple person, loving life, and those in it, but there are people that are special, people who have my attention. My kind of people.

Who are my kind of people?

They are the people who are kind and compassionate. They see life for what it is, understanding that in order to achieve, you do not have to tear others down, you can also achieve by lifting people up.

They are the kind of people who can function on their own, but are open and available enough to accept the love and help from another, not because they need it or to defer, but just because things are better when shared; not abdicated.

They are the people who know how to put themselves first, not because they are selfish, but because they understand if they are not stable and healthy, how can they be there for me? I know everyone needs a hand sometimes, and part of loving someone is being able to help them, not because they need saving, but because it is how I can help them grow.

They are the kind of people, who can laugh, enjoying a funny moment, even if it is they who caused the laughter. We all make mistakes, but to correct it and be able to laugh about it later with someone you trust, and who you know does not mean ill by the joke is a treasure, and there is nothing as attractive as a sense of humor.

The kind of people who know what love is and are willing to take a chance to accept it. We have all walked many paths, and had many false starts, but we should hold hope that things will work out, for if we lose Hope, then Pandora was holding the box for nothing.

Who are your kind of people?

Flaming June

flaming June with your hair as red as fire
your dress of embers
laid on a warm day at twilight
the sun holds no sway over you
dream your dreams
walk among the flowers of the field
without leaving your blankets
let the sound of the waves lapping at the shore
fill your mind as you slumber

where do you wander
that keeps you there so long?
does someone walk with you
in your dream state
perhaps holding your hand
whispering soft words
under the summer sun?

I will take your lead
my hair as red as the sunset
and lay as I dream, like you,
of whom I may meet
walking in their dreams too
a chance meeting in another world
where there are no rules
only emotion

Treasure

not all treasure comes in chests
caskets of wood bound with steel
held fast with lock and key
the most precious things cannot be held
behind gates or heavy doors
hoarded like a dragon lay on gold

the whisper in the night
the smell of your skin after making love
the way your hair falls at the side of your face
the creases at your eyes when you smile
the tilt of your chin when you laugh
these are my most precious treasures

A Glimmer of Hope

In the darkness
At the back to drawer
Where I keep my delicate things
The silks and the stockings
That need the most care
Is a little light
Shining faintly
Tucked out of sight
It's a glimmer that still glows
A glimmer of hope

Hungry

my fingertips trace your lips
and you take them in greedily
as we hold each other's eyes fast
devouring them
hungry for more
as though you have not feasted in an age

how do i know you are true?
how do i know you want me?
consent is everything
you are exploring, seeking
so, like a menu item you pick
you have to tell me

and there is no shame
for if you choose your words
then i will give myself freely
locking lips as we share breath
my fingers still wet
and i will have the taste of you on my lips

The Long Road

I would follow you like Moses
Let you lead me into a desert
tracking you for forty years
under a burning sun

I would stand on the shore of a sea
an enemy at our back
and trust you
to see us safely away

Brave hunger, loss, and despair
even when you are uncertain
and needing guidance yourself
waiting for a deliverance

Because, in my eyes you are touched
by the divine and I can only long
to be with you until my end of days
wherever that leads us

X Marks the Spot

there is ink under the surface of your skin
designs and patterns,
strange to me and disparate,
but they mean something to you,
a mix of uniqueness that makes you, you.

to me they are a roadmap
and i place a kiss,
tender and generous on each,
one by one,
following the road all over your body.

i love that your voice
is as loud as your skin,
unapologetic,
decidedly you, without hubris
you are as advertised.

what marks are on your soul?
what challenges did you face
that rebuilt you brick by brick
from the ground up, fresh?
i would love to know.

A Pause in Chores

I stopped what I was doing,
As I felt your chin slip into the crook of my neck,
And turning, I smelled the fragrance of your hair.
Your lips pursed in a gentle kiss,
I smiled, though you couldn't see it,
And pushed back into you, head thrown back
As your arms slipped around my waist,
Fingers meshed.
I would that I could stay like this forever
Yours to hold and to have.

Lantern

if I had a magick lantern,
one that conjured a jinn,
the kind with a single wish,
I know what I would do,
I would have it take my life,
    yesterday.

that is the day I lost you,
and I know that one wish is not enough
to have you back
and live everyday with you,
and a wish can't make love.

so, I would choose to give up my life
before we were parted
and that way I would never live
a single day without you,
my short life, would be complete.

Tears for You

Do you know why
I cry
I laugh
I live deeply
I hurt when you are in pain
I want the good for you.
Because I have a heart
Hot
Pumping emotion and blood
That the world
Hasn't
Quite killed
Yet

Make Me Want You!

Don't spare my emotions.
Show them to me raw, unfiltered.
Make me cry and scream,
But also,
Not for the sake of pity,
But for you and I.
Let there be laughter and joy,
Make me love you,
Because I can't ask
For your gifts,
Otherwise, they wouldn't be gifts.

My Friend of the Moon

You are amazing, as a person,
    an artist, and an inspiration.
Those who read your words know you,
Those who know you cannot help but love you,
For you are the Queen of Gothic to me,
Mistress of the Micro fiction.
I will enjoy your time,
One step ahead,
As others race to catch you up,
And when success comes for you,
And it will,
I will be able to say,
I saw that brilliance early,
And she was, and is still, my friend.

Prayers

When last I touched her
My fingers tips trailed over damp skin
The smell of sin was in the air
At least that's what they called it
I called it Sunday
For while they were all crammed into tight pews
Stuck in a drafty building that creaked
    when the wind blew
Praying to their God, and condemning
I was making love with my goddess
Whose prayers were answered first?

Terra Firma

I stand before you, small
my head in the clouds
as I dream of what could be.

Life is uncertain,
we know not where it will lead us
even when we think we've planned it.

Circumstance and fate
have a way of moving the path,
changing the course.

But you are my compass,
and I will keep a weather eye open for you
as I navigate my map.

Dangers abound,
as for Odysseus, homeward bound
as he sails his ocean return.

I often feel lost,
unsure if where I should be
and who I should be with.

But I look you to,
a guiding light, and inspiration
for confirmation of my journey,

Are my feet planted on terra firma?
Do I stand on solid ground?
Am I going in the right direction?

You are my Empress

On the day Romulus killed his brother,
A city was founded,
The seed of Empire planted.
I ask not for such grandeur
Or for blood to be spilled,
But I would have an Empire,
And at its head an Empress,
Seated on a throne,
An army at her feet.
For together,
We would conquer worlds,
Each of our own making,
In each other's arms.
Let no one stand between us,
Or against us,
Lest we strike them down.
Nothing can stand against love,
For it conquers all, and we are its proxies.

Songs

When I listened to the music
The gentle voice I admire
A strong woman who cuts her own path
Followed her dreams and worked her ass off
Spitting fire and flame to hold her ground
Mad, she cared when others didn't
I weep a little to hear her strength
Her fight
Her determination to carry on
And I thank those who think such of me
Because you are
My strength

I Can't

You wanted me to write you a poem,
but I can't, I'm sorry.
You are a not a few stanzas to me,
you are a sensory experience.

I want my eyes to linger on your form,
not on a page, a blank piece of paper.
I want my eyes to scrape over you,
every curve, every crease, every fold.

I didn't want to hold the pen,
I want to hold you, feeling the softness of your skin
as my lips press gently on it
planting small kisses over your body.

I want to taste the saltiness of you,
and the sweetness too,
as my tongue licks every part of you
from neck to feet, entirely.

I want to smell your tenderness,
that fragrance that only you capture,
the one that flashes my memory
when we are apart.

I want to hear you,
your whispers, your sighs, your moans,
as we lay together,
melded as one in love.

How could I write this?
I can only imagine what it is like
when we are apart and longing,
and I want you to imagine it too.

Curses and Prayers

My teeth pinched my lip so hard it bled, but I didn't feel it or care.

My breath whispered in first a curse as I was held on the threshold, frustrated, but when I tripped over it and the waves came, crashing over my body like a tsunami of flame setting fire to every nerve, breath slipped into prayers of gratitude, calling on god almighty, as my eyes rolled back in my head.

It had been so long, too long, since I had felt the pleasure envelop me so that my body sang, my hand still present, pressing the flesh in slow movements that ebbed with the subsiding satisfaction, an afterglow enveloped me as the pounding of my heart slowed and my breath became shallow again in my throat to couch silence.

Perhaps, I was not going to die after all. My mind cleared, peaceful and quiet once more. The whispers that had been constant and elevated to the pitch of screaming in recent days silent, satisfied for now.

As I regained my composure, I could taste the iron in my blood, a reminder that all must give way to lust, for it knows no master but that which it surrenders to for its own ends, to satisfy its hunger, and now I must recuperate, flushed and cooling.

Meet me in Eternity

Angels' fury
With fiery swords,
Defend heaven.
All nine chores deployed,
In service of a holy war.
Feathers bristle in flight,
As armies meet in battle.

Feathers and leather clash,
Swords ringing through the sky,
The hosts of Heaven and Hell locked.

When will victory come and what will it look like?
Only Heaven knows.
For in the end perhaps nothing will survive,
That could not fight for itself.

Mortals don no divine armor,
Carry no swords of justice,
We only have love to shield us.
A love for each other,
So delicate a thing that can be broken in a heartbeat,
So strong a thing that it can bear the weight of Heaven.

So, shield me in your love,
And I will shield you in mine,
Together we will weather this storm of fury,
This battle for the ages,
Our weapons to defend each other against all comers
Angel or Demon.

Burning for You

Draw me in and consume me
Like a fire that burns through wood
Take my body and my soul
For the fuel of your love
I don't care about the pain.

Whatever you throw at me would be worth it
I'll take the pain and transmute it
Into something shiny that I can present you
A gift of my suffering, if only to make you smile
For just a while.

I'll burn like a black sun
A hole in sky that absorbs all
Giving you my heat
However you need it
Burning for you

The Last Doves

When the last doves have flown south as summer passes, and the air is held still by the chill that freezes it, where will we be? There will be silence in those days, with no birds to sing in joy.

Will we be together, keeping each other warm, as though we are each other's suns? Will we be each other's voice, in speech and text, together apart? Or shall we be apart, separated by a distance too far to broach, still and silent like the air?

Will we be in each other's thoughts, buoying them to keep afloat, so that no storm, however severe, can touch us? The days stretch out before us, long and cold, even in the sun, but there can be more. More suns than the one that holds in the sky, unable to support itself the whole day through.

Our invisible sun can shine, day and night, to light the way, the dial always pointing to where it is.

Can you be a sun? Can you shine? Will you shine for me, as I would shine for you? Would you seek the doves with me?

Colors

My life is a kaleidoscope of color, a mix of confusion to even me.

Red hot passion
Only flows for
You in the long days that draw us out.
Given to sunshine kisses, I surrender
Beneath the copse of trees
In the springtime surrounded by
Verdant pastures, long grass smells of love.

White as snow when I join these colors together in a melding of light through the prism of hope.

You are a rainbow of colors to me, each a delight, each a mood, each a wish that I would plant on you with kisses, delicate as a flower.

Do not surrender the future based on the past, let this woman's hands lift you up, not in idolatry, but in support.

There are times when I will hold you, strong and determined, so that you stand tall.

There are times when I will need your strong arms to hold me, comfort me, as I would comfort you, sharing the burden of the other so that together we carry the burdens.

Atlas will look to us with envy that someone would share the load, for the love of each other, and not in deception as Heracles deceived him. Purity rare.

There is good in the world yet, and though I risk the fate of Cassandra to speak of the future, cursed to not be believed, there is time and hope for all, no one is forsaken by the past that still lives.

As we navigate this maze of emotion and life, scared of what might be and failure, I cannot offer you Ariadne's thread - but I can offer you my hand to take and hold, tight, while we walk together.

I will be your eyes and ears, as you will be mine, and we will share our breath in a kiss one day. Though I have no doubt there will be tears, I hope they will be of relief and happiness, a release, an offering, a cleansing.

So, deal with your life, live it, but don't lock me out and we will climb the highest point, after the deepest valley and share the view, wherever that may be.

The Mirror Has No Glass

The words arrive in the morning like dew on grass,
sweet and fresh, bringing my soul into the day
and I wish when you touch the first thing
    in your morning
that it could be me.

Distances can be traveled,
but finding a good heart is harder,
    and even harder,
for the best to accept themselves,
as I would accept them.

We all have our challenges,
but when you walk every day on broken glass
    and curse your feet,
all I can see is the strength and resolve
in still putting one foot in front of the other.

Though you doubt yourself,
    I do not.
When you cry,
    all I see is the power to let go.
When you say don't get attached,
All I want to do is hold you calmly
    even more, a rock, not a millstone.

An empty heart can be filled,
a broken heart, repaired,
a hardened heart, softened
    because I know you have one,
however much you deny yourself.

Gothic Beauty

Dark eyeliner and smokey eyes,
Burgundy lips curl softly,
Hazel eyes watching, mine grey

Time holds no sway over the gothic, drawn out like a waterfall that endlessly falls, never knowing an end, just a constant cascade of water plunging to crash in white foam when it hits.

Rocks are worn smooth, taking rough edges and rounding them so that they cause no pain, just a touch of the fingertips trailed over them in pure delight. There can be no resistance to water and time, they always take the roughness away.

Sunlight glitters in the water and a mist rises from the crash, little particles of moisture that shatter the light into its components to repackage it as beauty from the destruction, a rainbow of rebirth.

She moves through the room as though she is gliding like a ghost, not restricted to the floor, ethereal and haunting. The lace of her collar lays over the white blouse; a black choker tops it. The skirt held in place by the bottom of the crop corset, a vision of monochrome that resists color.

Shadows follow her,
As do eyes,
As she passes

Her mere presence is intoxicating, as she enters the room, heads turning quietly, she makes her way toward me. I can hear her breath as she gets closer, until she is close enough that I can hear her heartbeat, and she whispers into my ear. I am flame, burning in her presence, even though I am wet.

A pale hand, silver ringed, is placed over my heart, and she stares into my eyes, holding my gaze, fixed, as she feels my heart race, thunder in me, and she licks, her tongue rolling as she bites her lower lips and pulls it between her teeth.

I am losing my senses, my river runs, collapsing under her touch; burning for her, wanting to cry for her, wanting the breath to escape my own lips in low gasps as it gets louder, the pitch rising as a growl is trapped in my throat, unable to escape until she tells me it is okay to let go for her.

She consumes me,
I am helpless in her presence,
And I give myself freely

You Saved Me

You saved me from the night,
You saved me from the fight,
You let me lay silent in the dark,
As though it were a shroud that covered me,
Hiding me from the world.
You offered me a respite,
A place to rest my head, arms to hold me,
Keeping me safe in the night.
You held the tears back,
And then welcomed them with kisses,
When they came anyway.
You bathed me
In a love as sweet as honey,
As pale as asses milk,
And I became so smooth, soft as velvet
Under your gentle touch.
You taught me trust and vulnerability,
And what it was to be loved.
You showed me there is a better way
Than tearing at my soul,
A way of strength.
You're what I want,
All the days of my life
Don't make me wait for them to end
Before you tell me your truth,
I don't want to wait anymore.

Sacrifice

In magick, to know a things name is
    to have power over it
but the same applies in reverse
to know a things name is to surrender to it,
accepting it into yourself.

If you could crack open my ribs,
and examine my heart
you would find your name burned into it
a sacrament.

There is a music I hear,
horses, good, good, good horses,
and drivers in stockings, loving,
exciting me as the images play in my mind.

I would surrender myself,
return home,
because all good horses go home,
and be at peace in the act.

So, let the sun rise,
bathe me in light to cleanse my soul
making me worthy in your sight
and perhaps one day...

The Ship

Find me a ship for I must sail the ocean.
The journey will be long,
and the hardships many,
but I am drawn to sail, over oceans blue.
My heart aches to cross the water.

Find me a ship for I must sail the ocean.
The weather will be hard, not all blue skies,
so, the ship must be sturdy,
and the water is deep,
so, the hull must be strong if I am to survive.

Find me a ship for I must sail the ocean.
The journey will be cruel,
so, find me a crew who have hands to lend,
with backs breaking at the sail and ropes,
while I steer the ship where it needs to go.

Find me a ship for I must sail the ocean.
The journey will last a long time
so, I must have provisions.
Barrels of hard tack and water,
stored tight and packed with love.

For the need is desperate,
the urge to travel strong right now.
Out there in the world is the one I must find,
the one with whom I want to share tales
    of the journey,
so, for God's sake someone find me a ship!

Wind

My voice is a whisper on the wind
Traveling softly through the air
Moving silently over distance to your ears

My voice is a whisper on the wind
Carrying words of comfort and reassurance
Speaking of your value and skills

My voice is a whisper on the wind
I want you to have comfort and joy
For your days are long and difficult

My voice was a whisper on the wind
Talking of coffee and sunsets
The ordinary days of our lives

My voice was a whisper on the wind
That got closer with each passing day
Carrying a piece of me with it

My voice was a whisper on the wind
Sharing my feelings and soul
I would entrust them to no one else

My voice was a whisper on the wind
But now it is silent
It is your voice I long to hear

The Effects of Love

I hear the sound of music,
Painting images of light and dark in my mind,
The light and color,
Counterpointed
With shadow and shade
As the songs wash over my world.

And what is at the core of most,
But love, its gain and loss,
The thrill of its expression,
And the despair at its betrayal,
Blowing up the heart to full and beyond,
And I recognize the absence.

I would write a song of hope,
That I might find such pleasure and pain,
For although love cannot fill a void in myself,
It amplifies everything,
The softness and call of music,
The colors of paintings become more vivid,

And that's what love does,
It raises you up, making you more,
And that is why the fall is so great,
The topple to a personal hell,
A pit so deep and dark,
When heaven is withdrawn.

The Summer Isles

Take me to the Summer Isles,
Under the watchful gaze of Fae and fawn,
Where the Spring never ends,
Summer always on the horizon.

Take me to the Summer Isles,
On the boat across still waters
The reeds waving me goodbye,
As the candles burn for me.

Take me to the Summer Isles,
Where time holds no sway,
And my skin is as soft as morning light
That broaches a horizon forever misty.

Take me to the Summer Isles,
And let me lay in fresh grass,
The scent and sounds of you with me,
A blessing through dark times.

Take me to the Summer Isles,
Where the memory of you never fades,
As crisp and clear, as the first day we met,
And I still feel your kiss upon my lips,

For one last ride through fairy lands,
And through the kelpies and Jennie green teeth
    in safety I travel
Under the protection of the Elder,
As I travel alone to the Summer Isles.

The Shield

I am the shield that guards my heart,
The wall that stands in the way of hurt,
And the battle that rages in me,
Is the one that holds me up
While there is no other to do it.

I am the shield that rebuffs,
Turning back all approaches,
For no sword can touch that which
   it never gets near,
And so, the shield clashes and pushes,
Meeting all comers with resistance.

I am the shield that weighs heavy,
Pulling the arm that holds it down,
Matching the weight on the heart and soul,
Weary from the constant battle,
For an imagined hurt.

So, perhaps I should let my guard down,
Lower the shield that I have held,
For all these long years,
And let love take its chance,
To see if it can pierce the heart exposed.

Fingerprints

There is no denying the spirit
The Fire
The ghost of you
Held in the memory
So real that my skin
Displays the evidence of your touch
Burned by ice, welts of the fingerprints
You imparted on me
And on my very soul

Heartbeat

The rin tin tin of a beating heart,
The greatest timpani in the orchestra,
The sound to wake to,
Fresh from the womb,
And carried with us for life.
This sound knows no silence,
From first to last,
So treasure it with your final
breath.

Summer

When age catches me,
Fleet of foot, and out running me,
I will sit in the chair that has carried my impression
    for an age,
And think over the course of my life,
Dwelling on you.

In the winter of my time on earth,
When the days draw cold,
And my time wears thin,
I will sip tea and consider,
For there have been trials and tribulations.

But there have also been rewards,
That have filled my soul with sunlight,
The warmth and love of another,
And for this in the winter of the end days,
I thank you for being my summer.